PAT'S FLORIST

AN EXERCISE IN PRACTICAL ACCOUNTING

Frances Panich, EA
Sullivan County Community College

Cover image © Shutterstock, Inc.

www.kendallhunt.com
Send all inquiries to:
4050 Westmark Drive
Dubuque, IA 52004-1840

ISBN 978-1-4652-9180-6

Printed in the United States of America

Part 1

Pat Stone has established a reputation for her ability to create beautiful floral arrangements. During the last several months, she has acquired a large number of clients who use her services on a regular basis.

Following is a list of the transactions that Pat has had in her newly-formed flower arranging business that she's calling *Pat's Florist*.

Instructions: Using the worksheet provided, record each transaction **as well as the balances after each transaction.**

Sept. 1 – Deposited $ 40,000 from personal funds into business checking account.

Sept. 2 - Paid first month's rent of $ 1,200.

Sept. 2 - Purchased flower arranging supplies on account from City Florist Supply for $ 3,000.

Sept. 2 – Received $ 5,000 for a flower arranging fee.

Sept. 6- – Purchased and paid for Office Supplies in the amount of $ 750. (expense).

Sept. 9 – Paid $ 1,350 to a local radio station for advertising.

Sept. 12 – Paid City Florist Supply $ 1,500. on account for supplies purchased on Sept. 2nd.

Sept. 13 - Paid Utility Expense of $ 900.

Sept. 13 – Paid Telephone Expense of $ 625.

Sept. 15 – Earned $ 8,500 for arranging flowers for a wedding. The father of the bride paid $ 4,500 immediately and said he'd pay the balance next month.

Sept. 15 - Paid part-time assistant wages of $ 625.

Sept. 18 - Paid: Auto Expense of $ 650
Office Supply Expense of $ 500 Use 1 entry to record these 2 expenses.

Sept. 21 - Purchased additional flower arranging supplies on account for $ 3,600.

Sept. 29 - Paid $ 700 for flyers to be printed and distributed throughout the neighborhood. (Advertising Expense)

Sept. 30 - Paid part-time assistant wages of $ 575.

Sept. 30 – Took an inventory of supplies on hand (those remaining) at the end of the month and determined that their cost is $ 1,400. Thus, the cost of supplies used during the month is $ 5,200.

Sept. 30 - Earned $ 6,100 for flower arranging for a party. Received half that amount immediately and was promised the remainder next month.

Sept. 30 – Withdrew $ 3,275. from business checking account for personal use.

Name: ____________________

PAT'S FLORIST

Worksheet - Part 1

	Assets			= Liabilities	+ Owner's Equity										
Date	Cash	+ Accts Rec.	+ Supplies	= Accts. Payable	+ Pat Stone, Capital	- Pat Stone, Drawing	+ Fees Earned	- Advert. Exp.	- Auto Exp.	- Ofc. Sup. Exp.	- Rent Exp.	- Supplies Exp.	- Tele. Exp.	- Utilities Exp.	- Wages Exp.
9/1															
9/2															
Bal.															
9/2															
Bal.															
9/2															
Bal.															
9/6															
Bal.															
9/9															
Bal.															
9/12															
Bal.															
9/13															
Bal.															
9/13															
Bal.															
9/15															
Bal.															
9/15															
Bal.															
9/18															
Bal.															

Name: ____________________

PAT'S FLORIST

Worksheet - Part 1

	Assets			= Liabilities	+ Owner's Equity										
Date	Cash +	Accts Rec. +	Supplies =	Accts. Payable +	Pat Stone, Capital -	Pat Stone, Drawing +	Fees Earned -	Advert. Exp. -	Auto Exp. -	Ofc. Sup. Exp. -	Rent Exp. -	Supplies Exp. -	Tele. Exp. -	Utilities Exp. -	Wages Exp.
Bal.															
9/21															
Bal.															
9/29															
Bal.															
9/30															
Bal.															
9/30															
Bal.															
9/30															
Bal.															
9/30															
Bal.															

Total Assets ____________ Total Liabilities + Equity ____________

PAT'S FLORIST

Financial Statements

For the months of September - October

INCOME STATEMENT

STATEMENT OF OWNER'S EQUITY

BALANCE SHEET

Part 2

You have now completed the September transactions for *Pat's Florist*. The following transactions were completed during October, the second month of operations.

Instructions: Using the worksheet provided for, complete the following:
Enter the September 30th account balances in the General Ledger provided. (appropriate T accounts).
(*Hint*: verify the equality of the debit and credit balances in the accounts before proceeding with the next instruction.)
Journalize each transaction on the 2-column journal pages provided with the worksheets. **Be sure to provide journal entry explanations.**

Post the journal entry information to the General Ledger - individual T accounts. Using the page provided with the worksheets, prepare an unadjusted Trial Balance as of October 31st.

Oct. 1 - Paid office rent of $ 1,200.

Oct. 2 - Paid a 1-year insurance premium of $ 4,800 covering liability, theft and fire.

Oct. 2 - Pat Stone made an additional investment in her business by depositing $ 15,000 of personal funds into the business checking account.

Oct. 4 - Purchased a new computer and printer (asset) for $ 10,000 from City Office Supply. Paid $ 6,500 and put the rest on account.

Oct. 5 - Earned $ 6,500 for floral arranging. $ 2,500 was received immediately, the rest will be paid next month.

Oct. 9 - Paid for newspaper advertisement of $ 375.

Oct. 13 - Paid wages of $ 1,200 to assistant.

Oct. 15 - Received $ 4,000 for floral arrangements for a baby shower.

Oct. 16 - Paid $ 3,600 on account to decrease the Accounts Payable balance.

Oct. 18 - Pat signed a contract with a local florist for *Pat's Florist* to provide arrangements for the next 6 months, beginning in November, for a total of $ 15,000. In accordance with the contract, Pat received $ 5,000 as an advance payment.

Oct. 20 - Pat earned $ 4,200 for floral arrangements for a wedding reception. She received $ 2,200; the rest is to be paid next month.

Oct. 21 - Purchased Supplies for $ 7,850; paid $ 4,100 and put the rest on account.

Oct. 21 - Received the Accounts Receivable amount promised last month (on Sept. 15) from the father of the bride.

Oct. 24 - Paid:

$ 900 for Telephone Expense
$ 750 for Office Supply Expense — Use 1 entry to record this.

Oct. 27 – Paid Electric bill of $ 850. (Utilities Expense)

Oct. 30 - Paid Wages of $ 900 to part-time assistant.

Oct. 31 – Received $1,600 in payment for floral arrangements for a birthday party.

Oct. 31 – Charged $ 650 for Auto Expense for the month.

Oct. 31 - Withdrew $ 2,500 from business checking account for personal use.

JOURNAL

Date		Description		Debit		Credit

Date		Description		Debit		Credit

JOURNAL

Date		Description		Debit		Credit

PAT'S FLORIST

Date		Description		Debit		Credit
		Unadjusted Trial Balance				
		Cash				
		Accounts Receivable				
		Prepaid Insurance				
		Supplies				
		Computer / Printer				
		Accounts Payable				
		Unearned Fees				
		Capital				
		Drawing				
		Fees Earned				
		Advertising Expense				
		Auto Expense				
		Office Supplies Expense				
		Rent Expense				
		Supplies Expense				
		Telephone Expense				
		Utilities Expense				
		Wages Expense				
		Totals				

Part 3

Now that you have completed both September and October's entries for *Pat's Florist*, following are the end-of-period adjustments that need to be made.

Instructions: Using the worksheet provided for, complete the following:
Prepare adjusting entries from the information given below, **giving an explanation for each.**
Post the adjusting entries to the appropriate General Ledger (T accounts).
Provide an Adjusted Trial Balance.

a) Supplies on hand at October 31st were $ 4,000.

b) Adjust the Prepaid Insurance account for September and October.

c) Depreciation of the Computer Equipment for the 2 months is $ 250.

d) Wages earned, but not yet paid, at October 31st were $ 700.

e) On October 31st, Pat did floral arrangements for a large wedding. Her fee was $ 9,500 and was not collected by the end of the month. Provide the adjusting entry to record this income.

f) The Accounts Receivable amount recorded on October 5th was paid. Provide the entry to record this payment.

g) The Accounts Receivable amount recorded on October 20th was paid. Provide the entry to record this payment.

JOURNAL

Date		Description		Debit		Credit

PAT'S FLORIST

Date	Description	Debit	Credit
	Adjusted Trial Balance		
	Cash		
	Accounts Receivable		
	Prepaid Insurance		
	Supplies		
	Computer / Printer		
	Accoumulated Depreciation - Computer/Printer		
	Accounts Payable		
	Unearned Fees		
	Wages Payable		
	Capital		
	Drawing		
	Fees Earned		
	Advertising Expense		
	Auto Expense		
	Depreciation Expense		
	Insurance Expense		
	Office Supplies Expense		
	Rent Expense		
	Supplies Expense		
	Telephone Expense		
	Utilities Expense		
	Wages Expense		
	Totals		

Part 4

Instructions: Using the worksheet provided, complete the following:
Using the ending data from Part 3, prepare an end-of-period spreadsheet (work sheet).

Prepare *Pat's Florist's* Financial Statements which include the following:

Income Statement
Statement of Owner's Equity
Balance Sheet

Journalize and post the closing entries using the Income Summary account.

Prepare a Post-Closing Trial Balance.

PAT'S FLORIST

Worksheet - October 31st

Account Name	Trial Balance Dr	Trial Balance Cr	Adjustments Dr	Adjustments Cr	Adjusted Trial Balance Dr	Adjusted Trial Balance Cr	Income Statement Dr	Income Statement Cr	Balance Sheet Dr	Balance Sheet Cr
Cash										
Accounts Receivable										
Prepaid Insurance										
Supplies										
Computer										
Accum. Depreciation - Computer/Printer										
Accounts Payable										
Unearned Fees										
Wages Payable										
Capital										
Drawing										
Fees Earned										
Advertising Expense										
Auto Expense										
Depreciation Expense										
Insurance Expense										
Office Supplies Expense										
Rent Expense										
Supplies Expense										
Telephone Expense										
Utilities Expense										
Wages Expense										
Totals										

PAT'S FLORIST

Closing Entries

October 31st

Date		Account Name		Debit		Credit

PAT'S FLORIST

Post-Closing Trial Balance

October 31st

Date		Account Name		Debit		Credit

Part 5

Instructions:

Return to the adjusted Trial Balance totals in the General ledger (T accounts) in Part 4 and continue the journal entries described below. Add all new entries to the General Ledger (T account) balances after Part 3's adjustments.

In addition to arranging flowers. Pat has decided to expand her business and sell flowers, as well.

She now must purchase flowers to have in inventory as well as purchase flowers for a particular event. Pat has decided to keep track of her inventory using the **FIFO** method, as she will be using up the oldest flowers first to prevent as much spoilage of her flowers as possible.

Directions:

Make journal entries as indicated, **providing explanations for each entry.**
With each sale, be sure to charge Cost of Merchandise Sold and decrease the inventory using the **FIFO** method.
An inventory worksheet is included with this part so you can easily keep track of your inventory
All shipments are FOB shipping point; freight costs will be given with each inventory purchase.
These amounts will all be expensed to a Freight-In account.
Sales Tax at 8% is charged on **ALL** sales. *Be sure to make the appropriate entries.*

Nov. 1 - Purchased 3 groups of flowers:
a) 200 @ $ 1.00 each
b) 600 @ $ 2.50 each
c) 1,000 @ $ 5.00 each

Shipping charges (Freight-In Expense) is $ 200 and was paid for immediately.
For the flowers, Pat paid $ 4,700 and put the rest on account.
As the checks for the flowers and the shipping were to separate companies, separate checks were made out.

Nov. 3 - Sold ten arrangements using 300 of the newly-purchased flowers.
Total sales of the arrangements were $ 900. plus tax.
All were paid for in cash and one deposit was made.

Nov. 4 - Paid $ 700 wages to assistant. This amount was recorded as Wages Payable last month.

Nov. 4 - Paid Utility bill of $ 750. (Utilities Expense)

Nov. 5 - Paid last month's Utility bill of $ 750. This amount was NOT previously recorded on Accounts Payable.

Nov. 5 - Sold some more arrangements using 650 of the flowers in inventory.

Total sales of all the arrangements were $ 5,500. plus tax.
$ 3,000 plus tax was paid for and one deposit was made.
$ 2,500 plus tax was put on account and will be paid next month.

Nov. 6 - Purchased 5 groups of flowers:

a) 350 @ $ 1.50 each
b) 800 @ $ 3.50 each
c) 2,500 @ $ 8.00 each
d) 1,800 @ $ 6.50 each
e) 2,000 @ $ 5.00 each

Shipping charges (Freight-In Expense) is $ 1,250 and was paid for immediately.
For the flowers, Pat paid $ 15,000 and put the rest on account.
As the checks for the flowers and the shipping were to separate companies, separate checks were made out.

Nov. 10 - Pat's Florist received payment of $ 3,500. which was previously recorded on Accounts Receivable.

Nov. 12 - Pat paid the Telephone bill of $ 500. This was not previously recorded on account.

Nov. 14 - Sold arrangements for a wedding using 5,000 of the flowers in inventory.
Total sales of all the arrangements were $ 65,000, plus tax.
$ 30,000 plus tax was paid for and the rest will be paid for next month.

Nov. 15 - Ordered and paid for $ 675. of Office Supplies (expense).

Nov. 15 - Paid rent of $ 1,200.

Nov. 15 - Pat decided to purchase a van for deliveries (her orders were getting too big to be using her SUV).
She purchased a van for $ 45,000 and made a down payment of $ 10,000 at the time of purchase.
She borrowed the balance from the bank and set up a new T account called - Loan Payable, putting the balance in that account. She will be making loan monthly payments to the bank.

Nov. 18 - Received $ 1,500 plus tax for the sale of 100 flowers. All was paid in cash.

Nov. 23 - Purchased 3 groups of flowers:

a) 400 @ $ 2.75 each
b) 650 @ $ 3.00 each
c) 3,600 @ $ 4.50 each

Shipping charges (Freight-In Expense) is $ 875 and was paid for immediately.
For the flowers, Pat paid $ 10,250 and put the rest on account.
As the checks for the flowers and the shipping were to separate companies, separate checks were made out.

Nov. 24 - Pat paid $ 8,000 on her Accounts Payable.

Nov. 25 - Pat purchased $ 4,000 in Supplies and put it all on account.

Nov. 28 - Pat paid the Electric bill of $ 625. This was not previously recorded on account.

Nov. 29 - Pat checked her checking account on-line and found that $ 75. in credit card fees had been deducted from her account. Record this.

Nov. 29 - Make the adjustment to the Unearned Fees Account. (You have now earned 1 month of the prepayment. See Part 2 for more information, if necessary)

Nov. 30 - Pat sold arrangements using 6,000 flowers.
Total sales were $ 55,000. plus tax.
$ 29,000 plus tax was paid in cash; the rest was put on account.

Nov. 30 - Paid Wages of $ 1,000 to her part-time assistant.

Nov. 30 - Pat withdrew $ 14,000 for personal use.

PAT'S FLORIST

Worksheet - October 31st

Account Name	Trial Balance		Adjustments		Adjusted Trial Balance		Income Statement		Balance Sheet	
	Dr	Cr	Dr	Cr	Dr	Cr	Dr	Cr	Dr	Cr
Cash										
Accounts Receivable										
Prepaid Insurance										
Supplies										
Computer										
Accum. Depreciation - Computer/Printer										
Accounts Payable										
Unearned Fees										
Wages Payable										
Capital										
Drawing										
Fees Earned										
Advertising Expense										
Auto Expense										
Depreciation Expense										
Insurance Expense										
Office Supplies Expense										
Rent Expense										
Supplies Expense										
Telephone Expense										
Utilities Expense										
Wages Expense										
Totals										

Name: ______________________________

Date		Account Name		Debit		Credit

Name: ______________________________

Date		Account Name		Debit		Credit

Name: ____________________________________

Date		Account Name		Debit		Credit

PAT'S FLORIST

INVENTORY WORKSHEET

November

25	**Purchases**			**Merchandise Sold**			**Remaining Inventory**			Inventory Value
Date	Quantity	Unit Cost	Total Cost	Quantity	Unit Cost	Total Cost	Quantity	Unit Cost	Total Cost	
Beginning Inventory										
Totals										

Part 6

Instructions:

Continue the General Ledger accounts (T-accounts) you have in progress and add the following entries.

Bank statements for September through December are included in this packet. The statements for September and October are reconciled and are also included. You need to reconcile both November and December, and make any necessary journal entries resulting from these reconciliations. *Remember to use October's closing balances as your opening balances for November.*

Dec. 1 - Pat decided to set up a $ 300. Petty Cash fund for small purchases. Record this transaction.

Dec. 2 - Pat's Florist received $ 35,400 on previously recorded purchases (Accounts Receivable).

Dec. 3 - Purchased 3 groups of flowers:
a) 400 @ $ 1.50 each
b) 800 @ $ 2.75 each
c) 2,000 @ $ 3.25 each

Shipping charges (Freight-In Expense) is $ 500 and was paid for immediately.
For the flowers, Pat paid $ 7,500 and put the rest on account.
As the checks for the flowers and the shipping were to separate companies, separate checks were made out.

Dec. 5 - Pat paid $ 25,025 to decrease the company's Accounts Payable account.

Dec. 6 - Pat made a payment on her vehicle loan. The total payment was $ 1,250 - $ 1,000 was for the principal (the loan balance) and $ 250 was for interest expense.

Dec. 7 - Using cash from her petty cash fund, Pat spent $ 50. at the post office.

Dec. 10 - Pat sold 8 arrangements using 2,510 flowers in inventory. Total sales were $ 19,000 plus tax.

$ 11,000 plus tax was paid for and 1 deposit was made.
$ 8,000 plus tax was put on account and will be paid for next month.

Dec. 14 - Received payment on the Nov. 5th purchase that was put on account.

Dec. 15 - Paid Sales Tax Payable through the end of November.

Dec. 16 - Paid Telephone bill of $ 475. This amount was not previously recorded.

Dec. 20 - Received payment on the Nov. 14 purchase that was put on account.

Dec. 20 - As her supplies were running low, Pat purchased and paid for $ 6,000 of additional supplies.

Dec. 20 - For the Christmas holiday, Pat purchased the following flowers:
- Purchased 3 groups of flowers:
a) 2,500 @ $ 2.00 each
b) 5,000 @ $ 5.00 each
c) 4,000 @ $ 6.50 each

Shipping charges (Freight-In Expense) is $ 2,500 and was paid for immediately.
For the flowers, Pat paid $ 30,000 and put the rest on account.
As the checks for the flowers and the shipping were to separate companies, separate checks were made out.

Dec. 24 - 7,040 flowers were sold during the Christmas holiday.
Total sales were $ 52,500.
$ 37,500 plus tax was paid in cash.
The balance of $ 15,000 plus tax was put on account.

Dec. 26 - Pat paid $ 35,000 to reduce her Accounts Payable.

Dec. 26 - Pat took her assistant out to lunch. The bill came to $ 95 and was taken from petty cash.

Dec. 28 - Pat's assistant purchased a small amount of office supplies (expense) for $ 25.00 and took the amount from petty cash.

Dec. 29 - $ 135. of credit card fees were taken from the company's business checking account by Master Card and VISA. Record this transaction.

Dec. 30 - Pat paid her assistant $ 2,500 in wages, which included a year-end bonus.
Payroll information for the check is as follows:

Federal withholding was	$ 274.75	Social Security was	6.2%
NY State withholding was	$ 115.00	Medicare was	1.45%
Federal Unemployment was	.8 %	State Unemployment was	3%

Provide:
a) the payroll entry showing the gross payroll expense and related liabilities
b) the entry to pay the net payroll
c) the entry to record the payroll tax expense and corresponding liabilities

Dec. 31 - Pat withdrew $ 10,000 from the company's account for personal use.

Name: ____________________________________

Date		Account Name		Debit		Credit

Name: ______________________________

Date		Account Name		Debit		Credit

Name: ______________________________

Date		Account Name		Debit		Credit

Bank Statement

First National Bank
Anyplace, US
999-987-1234

Pat's Florist
Anyplace, US

Account # 36218

From:	September
Opening Balance	0
Deposits:	49,500
Withdrawals:	8,800
Bank Charge:	0
Closing Balance:	40,700

Deposits

Date	Amount
9/1	40,000
9/2	5,000
9/15	4,500

Withdrawals

Date	Amount
9/4	1,200
9/7	750
9/10	1,350
9/12	1,500
9/15	900
9/15	625
9/18	625
9/20	1,150
9/30	700

Balances

Date	Amount
9/1	40,000
9/4	38,800
9/5	43,800
9/7	43,050
9/10	41,700
9/12	40,200
9/15	38,675
9/18	42,550
9/20	41,400
9/30	40,700

Bank Statement

First National Bank
Anyplace, US
987-999-1234

Pat's Florist
Anyplace, US

Account # 36218

From:	October
Opening Balance	40,700
Deposits:	37,350
Withdrawals:	29,025
Bank Charge:	0
Closing Balance:	49,025

Deposits

Date	Amount
10/1	3,050
10/2	15,000
10/6	2,500
10/16	4,000
10/18	5,000
10/21	2,200
10/23	4,000
10/31	1,600

Withdrawals

Date	Amount
10/1	575
10/2	3,275
10/3	1,200
10/4	4,800
10/5	6,500
10/10	375
10/13	1,200
10/18	3,600
10/23	4,100
10/25	1,650
10/28	850
10/31	900

Balances

Date	Amount
10/1	43,175
10/2	54,900
10/3	53,700
10/4	48,900
10/5	42,400
10/6	44,900
10/10	44,525
10/13	43,325
10/16	47,325
10/18	48,725
10/21	50,925
10/23	50,825
10/25	49,175
10/28	48,325
10/31	49,025

September Reconciliaton

Book Balance		Bank Balance		
Beginning Balance	0	Beginning Balance		0
Deposits	52,550	Deposits		49,500
Checks written	-12,650	Withdrawals (Checks)		-8,800
Balance	39,900	Balance		40,700
Bank charge	0	Outstanding Checks	575	
			3,275	-3,850
Adjusted balance	39,900	Deposits in Transit	3,050	3,050
		Adjusted Balance		39,900

September entries:	Dr	Cr
Bank charges	0	
Cash		0

October Reconciliaton

Book Balance		Bank Balance		
Beginning Balance	39,900	Beginning Balance		40,700
Deposits	40,300	Deposits		37,350
Checks written	-27,675	Withdrawals (Checks)		-29,025
Balance	52,525	Balance		49,025
Bank charge	0	Outstanding Checks	2,500	-2,500
Adjusted balance	52,525	Deposits in Transit	4,000	
			2,000	6,000
		Adjusted Balance		52,525

October entries:	Dr	Cr	
Bank charges	0		
Cash		0	
			-

Bank Statement

First National Bank
Anyplace, US
999-987-1234

Pat's Florist
Anyplace, US

Account # 36218

From:	November	
Opening Balance		49,025
Deposits:		47,732
Withdrawals:		58,300
Bank Charge:		50
Closing Balance:		38,407

Deposits

Date	Amount
11/2	4,000
11/3	2,000
11/4	972
11/6	3,240
11/12	3,500
11/14	32,400
11/20	1,620

Withdrawals

Date	Amount
11/2	2,500
11/3	4,700
11/3	200
11/4	700
11/4	750
11/8	15,000
11/8	1,250
11/13	500
11/18	675
11/18	1,200
11/19	10,000
11/24	10,250
11/24	875
11/26	8,000
11/27	625
11/29	75
11/30	1,000

Balances

Date	Amount
11/2	50,525
11/3	47,625
11/4	47,147
11/6	50,387
11/8	34,137
11/12	37,637
11/13	37,137
11/14	69,537
11/18	67,662
11/19	57,662
11/20	59,282
11/24	48,157
11/26	40,157
11/27	39,532
11/29	39,407
11/30	38,407

Bank Statement

First National Bank
Anyplace, US
999-987-1234

Pat's Florist
Anyplace, US

Account # 36218

From:	December
Opening Balance	38,407
Deposits:	159,600
Withdrawals:	144,836
Bank Charge:	50
Closing Balance:	53,121

Deposits

Date	Amount
12/2	31,320
12/4	35,400
12/12	11,880
12/15	2,700
12/23	37,800
12/26	40,500

Withdrawals

Date	Amount
12/2	14,000
12/2	300
12/4	7,500
12/4	500
12/7	25,025
12/8	1,250
12/18	10,232
12/19	475
12/21	6,000
12/22	30,000
12/22	2,500
12/27	35,000
12/29	135
12/31	1,919
12/31	10,000

Balances

Date	Amount
12/2	55,427
12/4	82,827
12/7	57,802
12/8	56,552
12/12	68,432
12/15	71,132
12/18	60,900
12/19	60,425
12/21	54,425
12/22	21,925
12/23	59,725
12/26	100,225
12/27	65,225
12/29	65,090
12/31	53,121

November Reconciliaton			
Book Balance		**Bank Balance**	
Beginning Balance		Beginning Balance	
Deposits		Deposits	
Checks written		Withdrawals (Checks & charges)	
Balance		Balance	
Bank charge		Outstanding Checks	
Adjusted balance		Deposits in Transit	
		Adjusted Balance	

November entries:

	Dr	Cr
Bank charges		
Cash		

December Reconciliaton			
Book Balance		**Bank Balance**	
Beginning Balance		Beginning Balance	
Deposits		Deposits	
Checks written		Withdrawals (Checks & charges)	
Balance		Balance	
Bank charge		Outstanding Checks	
Adjusted balance		Deposits in Transit	
		Adjusted Balance	

December entries:

	Dr	Cr
Bank charges		
Cash		

PAT'S FLORIST

INVENTORY WORKSHEET

December

37	Purchases			Merchandise Sold			Remaining Inventory			
Date	Quantity	Unit Cost	Total Cost	Quantity	Unit Cost	Total Cost	Quantity	Unit Cost	Total Cost	Inventory Value
Beginning balances (from November)										
Totals										

Part 7

Adjustments at year end:

Instructions:

Following are the year-end adjustments to be made to the accounts of Pat's Florist. Continue the General Ledger accounts (T-accounts) you have in progress and add the following entries. Remember all adjustments are to be dated at year-end: December 31st.
Remember to provide explanations for each adjusting entry.

a. Pat counted the flowers she had in inventory at discovered she was missing $ 2,500 of her inventory. Record this information, reducing the value of the inventory.

b. Depreciate the: computer for another 2 months,

vehicle using the MACRS system, for 3 months or 1/4 of a year.
(See MACRS Chart at bottom of page)

Use 1 entry to record the depreciation for both items.

c. Just before closing on December 31st, Pat did several flower arrangements (**not** supplying the flowers) for a customer for $ 4,000 plus tax. The customer put the total amount on account. Record this.

d. Decrease the prepaid insurance for another 2 months.

e. The petty cash account was replenished for the amount spent. Pat counted the amount of the petty cash remaining and discovered the amount remaining in the fund was $ 140. Record the replenishment of the petty cash fund.

f. Supplies on hand at year end were $ 1,225. Provide the entry to record the remaining supplies and the related expense.

g. Pat realized she was not going to receive $ 1,800 in Accounts Receivable and would have to write the amount off. Provide this entry using the direct write-off method.

h. Adjust the Unearned Fees account for December.

i. Pat realized she forgot to pay the rent for December. She paid the monthly amount of $ 1,200.

Remember:

1. Your final inventory value on your inventory sheet has to match the inventory value on your year-end worksheet as well as on the Balance Sheet.
2. Your final cash balance should match the company's cash balance on the December bank reconciliation.
3. All Payroll Taxes and liabilities remain payable at year end.

Name: ____________________________________

Date		Account Name		Debit		Credit

Part 8

To complete the Project:

Using the worksheet provided, complete and submit the following:

DO NOT ROUND ANY NUMBERS.

1. A complete General Ledger (all T-accounts) showing all accounts used and their balances,
   including the year-end adjustments
   and Income Summary entries.

2. End-of-period worksheet, using:
   - the first set of columns for all balances,
   - the second set of columns for year-end adjustments
   - next the Adjusted Trial Balance
   - then the Income Statement information
   - and last, the Balance Sheet information

3. Income Statement, incorporating a statement of Cost of Merchandise Sold

4. Statement of Owner's Equity

5. Balance Sheet

6. Closing Entries

7. Post-closing Trial Balance

PAT'S FLORIST

Worksheet - December 31st

Account Name	Trial Balance Dr	Trial Balance Cr	Adjustments Dr	Adjustments Cr	Adjusted Trial Balance Dr	Adjusted Trial Balance Cr	Income Statement Dr	Income Statement Cr	Balance Sheet Dr	Balance Sheet Cr
Cash										
Petty Cash Fund										
Accounts Receivable										
Prepaid Insurance										
Inventory										
Supplies										
Computer										
Accum. Depreciation - Computer										
Vehicle										
Accum. Depreciation - Vehicle										
Accounts Payable										
Sales Tax Payable										
Unearned Fees										
Loan Payable - Vehicle										
Wages Payable										
Federal Withholding Tax Payable										
State Withholding Tax Payable										
Social Security Payable										
Medicare Payable										
Federal Unemployment Payable										
State Unemployment Payable										
Capital										
Drawing										
Fees Earned										
Sales										
Cost of Merchandise Sold										
Freight-In Expense										
Advertising Expense										
Auto Expense										
Bad Debt Expense										
Bank Charge Expense										
Credit Card Fees Expense										
Depreciation Expense										
Donations Expense										
Insurance Expense										

PAT'S FLORIST

Worksheet - December 31st

Interest Expense										
Meals Expense										
Office Supplies Expense										
Payroll Tax Expense										
Postage Expense										
Rent Expense										
Supplies Expense										
Telephone Expense										
Utilities Expense										
Wages Expense										
Cash Over / Short										
Totals										

PAT'S FLORIST

Financial Statements

For the months of September - December

Income Statement

PAT'S FLORIST

Financial Statements

For the months of September - December

Statement of Owner's Equity

Balance Sheet

PAT'S FLORIST

Closing Entries

December 31st

Date		Account Name		Debit		Credit

PAT'S FLORIST

Post-Closing Trial Balance

December 31st

Date		Account Name		Debit		Credit

GENERAL LEDGER

Name: ______________________________

ACCOUNT	CASH				
				Balance	
Date	Description	Debit	Credit	Debit	Credit

Name: ______________________________

ACCOUNT	CASH				
				Balance	
Date	Description	Debit	Credit	Debit	Credit

Name: ______________________________

ACCOUNT	CASH				
				Balance	
Date	Description	Debit	Credit	Debit	Credit

Name: ______________________________

ACCOUNT	CASH				
				Balance	
Date	Description	Debit	Credit	Debit	Credit

Name: ______________________________

ACCOUNT	ACCOUNTS RECEIVABLE				
				Balance	
Date	Description	Debit	Credit	Debit	Credit

Name: ______________________________

ACCOUNT	INVENTORY				
				Balance	
Date	Description	Debit	Credit	Debit	Credit

Name:________________________________

ACCOUNT	PREPAID INSURANCE				
				Balance	
Date	Description	Debit	Credit	Debit	Credit

ACCOUNT	PETTY CASH FUND				
				Balance	
Date	Description	Debit	Credit	Debit	Credit

ACCOUNT	SUPPLIES				
				Balance	
Date	Description	Debit	Credit	Debit	Credit

NAME:___________________________

ACCOUNT	VEHICLE				
				Balance	
Date	Description	Debit	Credit	Debit	Credit

ACCOUNT	ACCUMULATED DEPRECIATION - VEHICLE				
				Balance	
Date	Description	Debit	Credit	Debit	Credit

ACCOUNT	COMPUTER / PRINTER				
				Balance	
Date	Description	Debit	Credit	Debit	Credit

ACCOUNT	ACCUMULATED DEPRECIATION - COMPUTER / PRINTER				
				Balance	
Date	Description	Debit	Credit	Debit	Credit

Name: ______________________________

ACCOUNT	ACCOUNTS PAYABLE				
				Balance	
Date	Description	Debit	Credit	Debit	Credit

Name: ______________________________

ACCOUNT	SALES TAX PAYABLE				
				Balance	
Date	Description	Debit	Credit	Debit	Credit

NAME:________________________________

ACCOUNT	UNEARNED FEES				
				Balance	
Date	Description	Debit	Credit	Debit	Credit

ACCOUNT	LOAN PAYABLE				
				Balance	
Date	Description	Debit	Credit	Debit	Credit

Name:____________________________________

ACCOUNT	FEDERAL WITHHOLDING PAYABLE				
Date	Description	Debit	Credit	Debit	Credit

ACCOUNT	STATE WITHHOLDING PAYABLE				
Date	Description	Debit	Credit	Debit	Credit

ACCOUNT	SOCIAL SECURITY PAYABLE				
Date	Description	Debit	Credit	Debit	Credit

ACCOUNT	MEDICARE PAYABLE				
Date	Description	Debit	Credit	Debit	Credit

ACCOUNT	FEDERAL UNEMPLOYMENT PAYABLE				
Date	Description	Debit	Credit	Debit	Credit

ACCOUNT	STATE UNEMPLOYMENT PAYABLE				
Date	Description	Debit	Credit	Debit	Credit

Name: ______________________

ACCOUNT	WAGES PAYABLE				
Date	Description	Debit	Credit	Debit	Credit

ACCOUNT	INCOME SUMMARY				
Date	Description	Debit	Credit	Debit	Credit

NAME:____________________________

ACCOUNT	CAPITAL				
Date	Description	Debit	Credit	Debit	Credit

ACCOUNT	DRAWING				
Date	Description	Debit	Credit	Debit	Credit

NAME: ______________________________

ACCOUNT	FEES EARNED				
Date	Description	Debit	Credit	Debit	Credit

Name: ______________________________

ACCOUNT	SALES				
Date	Description	Debit	Credit	Debit	Credit

NAME: ______________________________

ACCOUNT	COST OF MERCHANDISE SOLD				
Date	Description	Debit	Credit	Debit	Credit

Name:_______________________________________

ACCOUNT	ADVERTISING EXPENSE				
Date	Description	Debit	Credit	Debit	Credit

ACCOUNT	AUTOMOBILE EXPENSE				
Date	Description	Debit	Credit	Debit	Credit

NAME:________________________________

ACCOUNT	FREIGHT-IN EXPENSE				
Date	Description	Debit	Credit	Debit	Credit

ACCOUNT	DEPRECIATION EXPENSE				
Date	Description	Debit	Credit	Debit	Credit

Name:______________________________________

ACCOUNT	INSURANCE EXPENSE				
Date	Description	Debit	Credit	Debit	Credit

ACCOUNT	INTEREST EXPENSE				
Date	Description	Debit	Credit	Debit	Credit

ACCOUNT	MEALS EXPENSE				
Date	Description	Debit	Credit	Debit	Credit

Name:________________________________

ACCOUNT	OFFICE SUPPLIES EXPENSE				
Date	Description	Debit	Credit	Debit	Credit

ACCOUNT	PAYROLL TAX EXPENSE				
Date	Description	Debit	Credit	Debit	Credit

ACCOUNT	POSTAGE EXPENSE				
Date	Description	Debit	Credit	Debit	Credit

NAME:______________________________________

ACCOUNT		RENT EXPENSE								
Date		Description		Debit		Credit		Debit		Credit

ACCOUNT		SUPPLIES EXPENSE								
Date		Description		Debit		Credit		Debit		Credit

ACCOUNT		CASH OVER / SHORT								
Date		Description		Debit		Credit		Debit		Credit

Name:______________________________

ACCOUNT	TELEPHONE EXPENSE				
Date	Description	Debit	Credit	Debit	Credit

ACCOUNT	UTILITIES EXPENSE				
Date	Description	Debit	Credit	Debit	Credit

ACCOUNT	WAGES EXPENSE				
Date	Description	Debit	Credit	Debit	Credit